VOCABULARY OF SILENCE

Books by Veronica Golos

A Bell Buried Deep (Poetry)

No Ordinary Women (Chapbook)

VOCABULARY OF SILENCE

POEMS BY

VERONICA GOLOS

RED HEN PRESS | Pasadena, California

Book design and layout by Andrew Mendez

Golos, Veronica
  Vocabulary of silence : poems / by Veronica Golos.——1st ed.
    p. cm.
  Includes bibliographical references and index.
  ISBN 978-1-59709-498-6
  I. Title.
  PS3607.O487V63 2011
  811'.6——dc22

                        2010049246

The Los Angeles County Arts Commission, the California Arts Council, the National
Endowment for the Arts, and Los Angeles Department of Cultural Affairs partially
support Red Hen Press.

Published by Red Hen Press
www.redhen.org
First Edition

Acknowledgments

Thanks to the journals/exhibits in which some of these poems appear: *Drunken Boat:* "Photo/Syn/Thesis"; *Meridians:* "For Fallujah", reprinted in *Contemporary World Literature; Pedestal:* "Snow in April (A Ghazal for Manadel al-Jamadi)"; *Pemmican Press:* "Unruly Alphabet", "Rain Song", "Bop(K)not: Juba! Juba!"; *Poetrybay:* "Voices", reprinted in *Contemporary World Literature; Press I:* "News of the Nameless", "Letter Damaged in Transit", "The City: Juárez:2010"; *Sin Fronteras/Writers Without Borders:* "Pietà"; *Squaw Valley Review:* "Snowy Egret"; *3poets4peace:* "Warrior"—translated into French and published in *Liqueur44* and *Verso*, Paris.

The Veil poems (those included here and others, thirty-eight in all) were part of a commissioned installation by the RANE Gallery in Taos, New Mexico. The poems (in altered form) were the basis upon which three visual artists—Deborah Rael-Buckley (sculptor), Robbie Steinbach (photographer) and Nancy Delpero (painter) created their work for the installation, titled *My Land is Me: Four Artists Explore The Veil.*

This collaborative multimedia installation delved into the idea of "the veil," a ubiquitous and iconic image with various and complex meanings in the East and the West. The artists explored representations of the veil with an eye to framing and re-framing and questioning the viewer's perception.

Veil poems appear in a catalogue book of the exhibition, *My Land Is Me.* (Blurb.com)

Poems from the Veil series were also part of a one-woman show by painter Nancy Delpero, which she inserted into her canvas.

Sky is everywhere; blue burqa sky was woven into an art project by fiber artist Faith Welch, displayed at a fiber arts show at the Stables Gallery, Taos, NM, in March, 2010.

I wish to thank Sawnie Morris at UNM in whose writing workshop many of these poems were first drafted, the *Squaw Valley Writer's Community* where some of these poems were written, and *A Room of Her Own Foundation* for the Creative Woman Fellowship to Ghost Ranch, Abiquiu, New Mexico where some of these poems were finalized.

Special thanks to Kate Gale and Red Hen Press, and to Dana Levin, Connie Josefs, Andrea Watson, Sawnie Morris, Summer Wood, Chris Brandt, Evie Shockley, Angelo Verga, Awista Ayub, Mary Crow, Nathalie Handal, Barbara Nimri Aziz, and Patricia Kenet for her generosity.

And finally, to my family, Jelayne, Jase, Belinda, Connie, Max, Molly, Jessica, and David: love and more love.

Table of Contents

PART TWO

BROKEN

VOCABULARY OF SILENCE

. . . *tomorrow*
(is) making its children. I hear their unborn voices
I am working out the vocabulary of my silence.
—Muriel Rukeyser, *The Speed of Darkness*

I saw a girl weep
without an alphabet, without a face.
—Saadi Yussef, *The Ends of the African North*

To become restless in the fixed place
to which we have been assigned.
—Edward Said, *After the Last Sky: Palestinian Lives*

FOR DAVID

HABIB

حَبيبْ

PART ONE
NEWS OF THE NAMELESS

Dream: The City: Baghdad, 2008

Who am I that I sit here at this door?
In my dream, there is a long alley, a place I learn *Want*.

The city is a mirror. Inside my reflection, old men are on fire—
Flaming like red kaffiyahs.

Litter ignites into funeral flares; the bread of the dead is baking.
Above the moans of children, soldiers warm their hands.

Avenues widen into downpour, detours unfold, flower into cemeteries.
Into this narrow place, two rivers clash.

Am I the one covered with brine, smelling of tides?
Or am I the stone, lifted like a flag?

Poem of Three

The Dead: *The year is a wound; the year is a yoke.*

Do you hear it? That drop, the snap of root? Stars wither, white grapes
burn. The sun stoops over the harsh mountain, and I am thirsty.

I pass through nothing and nothing is what I touch. Press me. I
am dire in the world.

The wordlessness of animals, I am between.
My throat is a grass plain, a foaming wind.

Lift this flap of heart, this gated rib. Ghosts live against me.
Tulips of fire.

The Soldier: *We are not going to give back any territory. Not in Baghdad.*

Here is the blank space, my fingerprint on the map;

at the nape of the neck.

I ride the pale horse until end without end,

a cloud of voices crying *don't*. My name caught

in the thread of a kill. I am charged.

The Witness: *At the end of sorrow is a door.*

The wind clatters. Eyes open. A beggar's bowl.
In the dank air, whispers. A shallow inside the sea, a mere syllable.

The tongue mute as a needle. A doll dancer
in a music box—a bit between her teeth.

News of the Nameless

⌐⌐

I climb marble steps worn to the shapes of waves.
I follow those with the loudest voices.

I am a dry broom
an old man sweeps his floor with; the sunlight speaks in Braille.

All Bethlehem is a child's tale: the crisis-crossed road,
the man in the white robe, the donkey,

the already dangerous dust.
Now the news is full of splinters.

Graffiti scars my palms, my wrists—
I walk through the library of forgetting.

I am my own news and nothing's
good.

⌐⌐

Who was he, naked and bound on the ground?
He is gone now.

Disappeared into the crowd of other news,
disappeared into someone's home,

where he sits, hands flat on the table—
pierced by a brilliant sun.

Where is the solider, the helmet, the hands, the threat
that pulled him naked from his cell

held him
as the choker clicked like a timepiece?

Who carries the dead weight, the iron cuffs,
the chair in the center of the room,

the whisper behind the earlobe?
I hear particulates strung along air, vibrating:

What is his name?
What is his name?

Voices

I am working under the voices of fire.

—Shareef Sarhan, Gaza

I was working under the voices of fire.
I was working in the night, bled white.
I was cracking open the shell to see inside.
I was sunning myself by the glow of shrapnel.
I was tunneling, tugging at something soft.
I was a tunnel
through which no one came.
I was the other end.

I slept only once in the bed of voices.
My shirt was woven of voices.
My home was built on the rubble of voices.
I planted green grapes in the black loam.

There were voices in our new names,
in the finishing rooms there were voices. So did
the harness, hood, shackles, broom handles have voices.
In the child the voices were spinning.
God was no-voice.

Photo/Syn/Thesis

⟲

Leash. Hand. Leash. Hand. Leash.

Look at the photo. Take-a-pin+stick-it-through-the-figures. Puncture
to let
light in.

Still, you
must mar the surface—scratch the image
must get inside\

as if you could

enter

the cement ground the narrow hall the stink.

The photo   for *us*   is
First Cause.

⟲

See.

The woman is pale, strange, standing, her head to the side, holding
the leash
the naked man lying dark
on the floor, his head twisted, without name even though they call him
Gus, like a gust of wind, or dis gus ting, or dust, dust he shall
be . . . she has a name, *Lynndie.*

See our own hand holding a *thing*—*leash*—our eye traveling
the length of our own arm—to the delicate 8 wrist-bones spread of 5
fingers—the great one thumb—opposable—off-shoot of thought—
a maker's hand—that which makes us
human—a handhold—but—
loose or tight—the hand holds

the
leash.

⟿

if by accident or the occult   I (eye) could stop
the virtual ones + zeros anxiously replicating
bend back to before before

that man (image) naked on the cement ground
there were meadows covered with human skin under the Arabian moon

his skin torn scraped his face blurred with such
pain   could it be

lifted out from him as if ripped from the image of his image of his image?
If re-genesis were possible   if the pain itself became

the woman *not holding the leash*
but emptying out of herself

if only I could steal back that

electrical pulse
inside the camera   (infinite) if doing

so could eradicate
what happened

but it did happen,

because
it did

the photo is there:

⌁

The dark thick fabric of the underneath.

You know—and I know—it is—

within me—within you.

Vocabulary of Silence

⌒

Love, what is your other name?
Who rides the red horse, the one that is smoke?
Who tramples the fields where words are tinder?

What makes us? I want it to be Love.

Come near
the naked man. A hood—over his head. His hands—tied behind him.

How to utter it?
What word could open my jaw?

Tanks bullets drones   air-strikes   starvation sanctions structural
adjustment programming poisoned land police truncheons torture harsh
up collective punishment   cigarette burning   water-boarding

My tongue splits.

⌒

From the red sea, from its salt water, from its warm shallow shoals,

 . . . Behold!
Here are my good . . . dead
rising!

They rise between river and river, between sword and sword.
They rise between the hour of song and the hour of work
between the echo and its saying. They rise inside
the cup-shaped hollow of pelvis—they rise and ripen and never grow old:

*Mohammad Omar Jawad Ali Selma Madia Fatima Suhad Hussein
Ahmed Salam Azad Aysha Maysoon Nuhad Faisal Raad Zaid
Widad Nuha Haifaa Amal Kifah Souad Fallujah Ramadi Diyala
Basra Gaza*

My day is a froth out of which the dead rise,
these particular dead, the ones who come every morning in the middle of prayer.

They cushion my knees and follow my hand movements.
They are residue in all that I drink.

I place my forehead to the floor.
I fumble with the lyric, move my finger as a blind person

along its calligraphy.
It is written: I am cause—and comfort.

Cost of It

Go beyond the past tense into the present.
They brought me a foot
and a carved ear, and told me
these were my enemies. *Eat this*, they said.
Flesh meets in my hands.
My teeth are scythes.
They said, *You are emptier than air.*
Now I pull hurricanes from mouths of the dead.
Now I crow, crawl into the pit of those
who spare me nothing.

Frag—
ments

⌀

A waxed seal. If you break it open,
under your gaze
meaning crumbles.
That's what *infidel* means.

⌀

War—
its absence—a trick
of light, blinding—
like the Interrogator's lamp.

⌀

Names of the dead slur between tongues,
mispronounced: sudden: wasp
in the throat:
Say what I mean you to say.

⌀

Derelict souls shipped out
shipped back
as cargo.
Their truth is silence,
that cold cage, that bullet.

The City: Juárez, 2010
(The desert and wind speak)

⁓

DESERT:

I've worn my girls down to bone,

Alma, Angelina, Jessica, Luz, Elizabeth, Veronica, Ivonne,

muted their last awful begging, their last

scream embedded in their arms, their delicate wrists, their circle of ankles.

I've known them. Intimate,

I've rubbed against their hips, nudged their throats, found

a place for myself inside their curves.

Maria, Donna, Lorenza.

My voice is a rasp, it smoothes

and smoothes

till they are only fragment—

Esmeralda, Emilia, Guillermina.

A white shirt. A short black skirt. One blue shoe.

WIND:

I've come with my one song, *Maquiladora*—

a refrain drenched in their sweet sweet

sweat.

Gloria, Adriana, Karina, Ignacia, Laura Ana, Gabriele,

I've hummed it to them again and again,

come, come I said . . . as if I were

Silvia, Dora, Juana, Rosa, Clara's

self.

DESERT:

Here, take this.

For Josephina,
this bite
etched into her long bone of leg.

For Claudia,
this bottom jaw, splintered.

For Alejandra,
this tunnel of ribs, flattened.
My lovely carved ones—my *Santa Muertes.*

⟋⟋⟍

WIND:

Susana, Miriam, Beatriz, Janeth, Iris, Estela, Diana,

through the flutes of their bones I drone

Dominus, Dominus Vobiscum, Dominus, Dominus Vobiscum . . .

I carry each—each woman's name—to you—to you—

⟋⟋⟍

DESERT:

I am the boneyard
of bracelets, the torn slip,
the broken nose, the pleadings,
the purse, the ankle-strap, the acid,

the wire, the rope, the stockings, the bludgeon,
the knife, the bullet, the semen, the spit, the slit,
the drowned, the blow, the burn, the electric torch,
the spinal cord broken, the lye thrown in the face, the steel
drum, the belt, the trench, the ditch, the car, the naked from the waist
down, the raped, the shot, the raped, the stabbed, the 14, 25, 18,
34, 50, 10 year old, the unknown, the working girl, the mother, the daughter,
the sister, the wife, the *voces sin eco*——

EDEN IS RUIN

Warrior

My past washes back, a low tide,
a haunting song.

Like the zing of the arrow
sound has a shape.

Flesh. There will be war.
Witness. Stand on the field

as the ones who are already dead
need you to. Stare. Never let go.

One can not measure
death. I know—

I am the one who cuts—broken
as the edge of your cup.

See—the bow I have become, the bones, the arrow—

man, but not a man.

Snowy Egret

(after Bruce Weigl)

It was the world, fusing
and alive that pulled the
boy out. Wrapped him in

skin—forever a pearl out
of shell. He was without
shelter the way we sometimes are;

only the *blue face of*
the pond opened inside him.
The egret's there, always in

the pale morning, mist rising
off it like a robe.
The boy goes there with

a gun——

       because.

The egret was born first
like snow, foggy and fragile.
Something of birth always clings,
refuses even as it pushes

so that to become what
you were made to be
the body must conjure out
of the kiln of air

and slateblue shallows, what turns
leg and beak black, leaving
for the last, a stain
of yellow for the foot.

The egret now is grown.
Full and feathered, lacey plumes
a spread of white inside
a denser white. The boy

watches it go to wing,
circle, tilt into blue, then
unfasten into the wet shadows
below.

Boy. Gun. Blank Sky . . .

Cain/
Qayin/
Qabil

It
always at me
pressing
wanting
pulse

     It
     scratched me from the inside
     once cut/ i could not heal

knowing——desire   sharpened upon a rock

something twisted
    here here here
i found the word——uh uh uh uh   *no*

when then brother
laughed/cut   the living
     lamb/ with stone
lamb   was not

It
no longer
inside the life/lamb

and

there was on brother this red
his wrists
 \ hands blurring in-side the blue
air
smoking

It   a voice

an itch always   upon my skin

for   It
        i built earthmud
mound
        all was
green
            giving
            for me   to give

brother laughing

and

after
earth would not
yield
my hands   could not gather
i wore out my soul
digging

brother
above me/hill
sang
sound wove yellow through leaves
light
sang

It
poured
whirling
windwhite
breathing
Yes

It
burrowed in brother
Yes

i only wanted
to go

beneath
I only wanted to know what i did not know

and

i opened brother
i opened brother
i saw inside
It
shining
larger
      than star
It
      unfurling/bursting/becoming

then

  It
      came at me   noise against noise
 clanging banging again against me
      It covered my hands the red smell/taste
of brother on my fingers in my mouth
      It was in me loud so loud   It hurt
     what   i asked   what

am i/am i/ am i my/ am i my brother/am i my brother's
keeper

and

mountain broke itself into rocks
lamb/brother broken
sky broken
field broken too
i broke

every   thing

exile

            the angel hissed

    at the gate of fire

                        my hand went through it

            its name(s)   long in my mouth

        ooooooooooooooooooooooooooooooo

    please   i said

        i only want   to know

            Y   M   I

44

now i am
here

                          sent

to be
           before
you

Letter damaged in transit

Dear Da   d

I just wa   nted to write you before I   can't   this up   you

what   I've do   ne   here in Ir ag

and then   yesterday another soldier in my   squad

took s poon

brains   laughed dead Iraqiii ~~there's a photo~~

~~arm around the corp~~ ~~so~~ ~~it wasin Camera~~

the family his brot   andfather witnessed   w

e afroached one house in   far ming area, Mosul I think maybe ..family..*i*//dog   so much

bloodthreechild

Dad.. .000.. .. .. sss   not what I

thought

midnight raids on Kirkuk, Samara, Bhagdad Mosul Tikrit

I   can't   any///mo!re

to   shreds. Here's how we do it, you run in and if there's

One rifle team outside grab man of the

house...sofa

"wake em up!"""

caped . 110 degrees   I mean farm   out skirts   of Tikrit

we the xxxxxxxxxxxxxxxxxx

screams

not what I join   ed t   o   do   a few kids and old man

can't Dad   peeing on themselves   rules of en   gage

ment?   Due   pressure   head split o pen

ope n bo——dy bags   de   sec reating   abu ghraib   Dady   you

don't

what   if

know

if\who   enemy   ?

Pietà

What of the farm mother, her soldier son, shattered.
She hides her shuddering inside the closet, rubs the coat
and boots he'll never need again——his body of cut-off-stems.

Before, in his childlife sleep, his legs flung open, sometimes
she couldn't even look he was so beautiful, although she didn't have then,
and doesn't have now, the word——

She's speared through——
that smell in his room
his blind left eye,
three limbs sawed away
his shit staining
the white sheets——

the Wal-Mart sheets she buys and buys . . .

you see he had been
so crisp, so cut-line, so formal in the uniform,
as if he had been pressed somehow
inside and

her with her deep knowledge of ironing,
of pressing herself,
had recognized it in him, you know,
and saw beauty in it, yes,
in the sharp crease, it was clean and clear, that work
of hands and
the message that work carried,
that someone had done this for him.

She rolls him on his side, and removes, four times daily,
the sheets from his bed, daily, brushes her fingers
against his white tee shirt lightly (its short arms flap, there is nothing to hold)
finding muscle there in his still-strong back,
and the back of his head that little scar

from the day he fell off the tractor, when she thought yes I could kill
I could kill his father, yes for this, *oh*—

Her memory is a sharpened thing.

where where are his arms and his leg

she wants to lift him, she wants to smother him, she wants to finger all the edges
of his wounds, she wants him back, she wants him to die. All her words, the ones
she could say on some spring day *the sun's out   the rye is up*

stuck
somewhere below the solar plexus of her
those beauty words *sun grass rain horse earth*
gone—

only he remains

THE SILENCE

For Fallujah

~⌒

Words spool into concertina wire, punctuation wounds. Three
tiers deep, the wire awakens to pursue its hurt. Each day
is a membrane to puncture and pass through.

I offer grief. I know its gravity.
At the graves, the names of the dead are scribbled into dumb air.
I thread letters into vowels, scratching at their script.

Five times the clarion call. Five times the delicate skin of sound is stretched,
and the cry, *Allahu Akbar!* trembles into ululation,
as the layered nameless resurrect into

song. O survivor: Your voice is disjointed; your tears are music too. I know
not what to do. I emerged from the sea
and pulled the trigger.

The finger points. No. Don't show me the bruise—the brilliance
of bombs robs night of its color. Touch and sight go numb. I turn away.

~⌒

Sunset. A red
that kindles in the body. A lantern
beneath water,

53

something swallowed,
seen through, and there at molten
core

a word
that does not
hold. That will not
grip.

Our hands
can do—nothing.

Birth(ing) Word

~⁀ɔ

I emerged a zero howl of infant seconds pressing towards the aftermath of echo; I
vibrated into declaration. At my outermost edge,

I was grafted, spun into what is translated; the lip which spoke me was mountain,
the sea, vowels I wept out—

I was strung between each song, a thin waft, corrected into web, a bleached participle,
enunciation and annunciation, the spoke in the wheel of glass, I dilate, vitreous, fevering
into form.

~⁀ɔ

Now, this blue. Blue burst from a tuber throat, from the larynx, the great *babyblue
exhalation of the one god*, the barb inside the breath.

Listen. Whole flesh *out of what ceases into what is ceasing*. I am already transparent, already a
shimmer, an aperture leading into aperture; then for a moment—still—solid—a passage.

". . . on the palms of My hands have I graven thee." Carved word to flesh to form
to curvature to sky to land. Not yet ink, only pen, only *axis mundi*.

Stained mottled eyelid, city of fingers, a thumbprint blurred,
not yet, not yet—congealed—into script.

~⁀ɔ

How am I to live? Vernacular, segmented?
Vertiginous? Am I not whorls on a thinking thumb, the cellular split?

What is it to be human?

There is something in me the sparrow knows,
the sky of space and blue,
belonging to a place

in the slippage. Between the spaces

I cut
to find, as a child would, what is inside:

It is nothing I tell you.

Un fa ith
full

........................)silence(

Somewhere between us *silence* moved,
trembled, was not
transparent. The place into which our words
tumbled. The space into which our letters
dissolved, remixed to code;

silence wasn't what we meant, it seems.
Silence was fixed—even with an oiled
hook, nothing lured words back from it,
once dropped into. Signs came and went
inside. Something swelled; we didn't want
knowing
to-be inside (me), because
knowing
would scrape down, and

silence would take and take
as if eels slipped down its throat, a throat so
deep with awe all we had left multiplied into
answers we didn't want

to question. What was said then wasn't ours
anymore, but *silence's* third thing,
that rang and didn't stop, even at dinner; yet
every tone was known, you knew and I
knew

too. So *silence* was it, and not the words or
what words might mean, or what was
underneath words—after all words weren't

at fault, what was done was done because
words weren't there, at all, and *silence* had
grown so large it had to be filled
with something; so it began, not that words
are left to tell it, but

be-cause

. . .

Sumeria

⁓

—shot through with spark

lamps that light themselves

they burn they burn they burn me.

—the women are intricate knots.

Have I the courage to walk
                   through their terrible gaze?

Their feet are nailed with restlessness.
Their home is a tunnel of sighs—a nourishment of grief.

⁓

A charged light—

              a silk chador
                          slips beneath my eyelids.

Stuffing my mouth is a silence that removes all silence:

In this garden black flies swarm
        my palms flare
fingers splayed
        spikes against rock.
            —I am being taken—
                the wall I press against pressing back.
            What climbs me—clinging and feeding—continues and—
            neither the blank shade nor
the clanging air
        can stop its vertical dig upward—can halt the ushering in—
                            I am the core through which the bullet fires.

Poppy 13

⁓

The train's gun-metal thrust through the iron stem of tunnel
out past a sudden crimson
blur—
—the world outside the hurtling compartment is not
solid, only florid.

⁓

Palms the color of poppy, open. At the center,
a bitter coin—stop.

⁓

Their black eyes—wine-red lashes—stare—I am the one
rooted—and they—are moving—shallow—sly—but moving.

⁓

Incise the green capsule—at the line of wound lip, a gush of milk
a nipple slit, through which I sip
the white reverence, bring forth *somniferum* . . .

Mazur-i-Sharif, Badakhstan, Jalalabad—

residue.

Up close, the fun-house mirror
plagues the sighted—dirt beneath fingernails—rain on the petals:
a poppy in white and black and wet—

 Glossy heart. Quick god. Crucible.

The wild refuses the curvature of vase.

Entourage of spiked leaves.
And hunger—needed—so the poppy will lean
outward and toward, will cling, nestle into the driest dirt,
rock crevice, topping our walls: What is broken? What is ruin?
Its milk is a premonition.

~⟶

Lucid fire-color, eruption stilled.

Short-lived anemone of sunspots.
Furious rake, saw-toothed manacle,
vivid summer sheen—

~⟶

When Balance (Libra) makes the hours of daytime and sleep equal and parts the world in twain (August)...then is the time to hide in the ground your crop of flax and the poppy of Ceres. —Virgil, *Georgics*, 1.28

~⟶

Sow among the corn—poppy, delicate musk of between—where I long to be.

~⟶

Use fine sand. After the snow melts.
Or on the ides of March. Plant the gaudy flash

in the morning. Shallow holes, the dibble stick.
Toss from your hand in that ancient arc:

One acre, one pound of seed. Plant.
The moon will tow. Shadows ripen its blood spilling seed.

Now with hammer and spike,
        drive deep into the laid track, break
the tines of the road that took us far from home:
        the needle, the pipe——the floret of pain needing assuage.

After

A Ghazal after Agha Shahid Ali

Do we have a home, O Prophet of Mercy, born of the Nile? Exile
is no place of return. Your eyes and palms never rest while in exile.

Born here. What land is mine, when all was taken from another?
My foot scorches the hills. Here, even the dust's afire with exile.

Was not Eden our exile too? "You were exiled by exiles,"
said Shahid. Earth refusing us. Now we conspire to exile.

Imagine famished for place. The nectar of home.
Everything lost. This: "a fashion of fire" in exile.

These landscapes: mountain, mesa, unrestrained sun. Rivers speak
a language I've never learned. Language is always wilder in exile.

"The air is vinegar . . ." It startles, wakes us from trance;
the one who is wounded, spins, spins in a gyre of exile.

"A curfew of water". Clandestine, I walk the Reservation's hill;
voices pour down like hurricanes—voices acquired in their exile.

What requires me then to offer, "my heart silk-wrapped"?
It's the sting of chords—that chorus—the choir of exile.

Now the god of exile explains. Says my name: *Golos* means exile.
Mountains, even the skies, cry *Leave!* The gods never tire of exile.

PART TWO
BROKEN

First Veil

In the beginning we were bedecked like orange trees, a garden flowering.
Color, even lilac. Sound of intones, the voice of one, murmuring.

Bop (K)not: Juba! Juba!

problem . . . roses. You're hanging the just-washed clothes in the stringent sun,
the hollyhocks sigh their deep sighs as they lean their heavy stems against the wall,
the first lavender iris has come and gone, the russian sage is sunning itself. The wild
roses multiply, base and prickly, their bunched pink faces exhale a perfume to make you
giddy as you flip the wet sheets over the ropeline you've strung from fence to tree.
The birds are almost speaking. You are happy. *Juba!*

> *Juba*: A city in southern Sudan on the While Nile River;
> formerly, in the American South, a lively rustic dance with much "clapping and
> thigh-slapping," the word *Juba!* repeated as a refrain;
> Happiness—

an *elaborate* flounce, lacey twirl-swirl soft plated spin-spiral pine design of overlap:
the Golden Mean. I mean: I part the leaves of the flower,
lift one then another & another to find the seam, flotsam of my dreams,
Juba—Juba!
and there she is, the girl running to me, her face of chaste petals
tearing, her puregirl *mons venus*-bomb-napalm-photo-run—
I am strung
between *Juba!* and sorrow-song—

> *Juba*: A city in Sudan on the White Nile River;
> in America's South, dance with much "hand clapping, thigh-slapping," *Juba!*
> repeated;
> Happiness—

the brazen sun revolving, stroking and spilling over me & the wide-mouthed poppies,
the buzz-hum iridescence of birdwhirling—what rises here I can barely name, how is
it possible, this *Juba!?*   No—*nong qua! nong qua!* her Vietnamese girl-voice
clicks, *too hot too hot*—no—I say back, I love the sun—*nong qua! nong qua!*
she moans—I turn—I can't turn away—she is here in my garden . . .
how will I turn back—*nonq qua!*—how? to my *Juba!* again?

    Juba: Sudan. White Nile. Dance, clap *Juba!* Repeat.
    Happiness—

Second Veil

~~

Someone is before me, someone is behind me. We
open and are passed through as if we are water, as if
we stand in a pool and flower, growing wide in the sun—

~~

Her face is unexpected earth.

~~

Veiled in rain.
Inside—looking out.

Rain Song

. . . it's raining thick gray New York rain—rain that fills the gutters that soaks my coat
seeps down the back of my neck and when I finally climb on the bus the rain is steam

rising off my shoulders, the bus driver has his hands on the large wheel, is urging the
huge animal of the bus forward is stroking the wheel whispering or praying as we make

our way through the pouring, the honk and screech of traffic muted, we are all swaying
in a steamy bus the light begins its change from red to green—look

at the passengers, our faces are beginning to blur, as if there is a crying rising in us, as if
we are being filled with rain, rain is tapping on our organs, is filling

the crevices of our lungs, liver, heart, heads and our craniums, the eight bones
of the wrist, our particular fingernails; the rain outside is carrying on, is almost wild,

pouring itself into the world, wordless and troubled, and we who are almost sheltered
in this steam and fog and huffing bus, the earth in us is rising, as if the rain is wearing

us down to humid dirt, as if we could begin again, perhaps we could change,
become someone else, empty our pockets, change

our clothes, hair, the color of our skin, become a man, woman, grow to childhood
again, or age so quickly our bones would be made of light and we would glide

down the rain-soaked streets, the gleam of rain still on the tar, on the huge billboards,
the streetlights surrounded with halo, night coming on, and the stars and moon

would be bright and clean and pure and there would be no war, and the hungry
would be fed, and the children loved, as we would be loved, and oh,

life is good and will be different, won't it, won't it, when we step off the bus in the rain.

Third Veil

"Watch where you go!"

In my dream, an overrun garden, a carved face of a woman, her hair writhing
with stems. Moss forms a mask, foaming and alive.

On the ground, fragments of clay. I lift one to my tongue. It tastes
of salt. I gather its shards into my lap,

as if I were going to make a bowl,
using what is broken, as potters do.

Unruly Alphabet

⸱⟋

Call Caroline. Check with Connie about Carmel, California.
Cauliflower's on sale at Cid's. Buy skinless chicken for lunch.

The days glue together,
though not in any alphabetical order I understand,
but they do seem to be writing something.
Last week, for example,
was filled with E-F days: eat nothing but vegetables, exercise,
elaborate, make an excuse—
finish the baking, find the sunglasses, mark
final exams, flip the tarot card over . . .

What is the message? Perhaps my days are being written
in a non-Romance language, with q's and y's and
z's mixed in the center of their words; or they end
in clicking x's, o's and i's? Perhaps they are tapping out
a code?

⸱⟋

But then:
My blouse grows.
The walnut refuses its light.
Wooden crosses decked with pink and yellow plastic flowers
        align themselves in my driveway.
The round lake
is hungry;
people are in pieces, living as if at the end

of diving boards; bird people, standing on one leg, or on one arm,
fluttering feathers, gold feathers; fear
like a transparent gauze, or like a glaze
of a donut, sticky on your fingers, its taste
sweet.

I have to pack, hang the photos, phone 10 people, pick the peaches,
cut the peony; the plumber and the police are due.

The walnut has a brain, loose
inside the shell. When you smash it, it stops thinking.

Who cracks open
the head of another human?
What is inside
a person who does this?
Perhaps nothing. Perhaps when they were young,
someone else shook them, tipped them
over and out
and, through their eyes,
ears, nose, mouth, from under
their finger and toe nails—poured out everything they were?

Everything being what is impossible to list or know or alphabetize,
since we're always forming:
        like the forest turning green
overnight, or ice on black bark.

      ~⊃

Did you know: There are cemeteries under water?
How do the bodies stay down? you ask.
They don't, they dissolve. That fish you're
eating? Don't worry, it's probably
from a place where there are no cemeteries, a part
of the world where bodies haven't
been dropped from helicopters,
drowned while crossing an ocean in a raft from here to there to here,
or drowned tied to a chair in the middle of a pitch-black room:
        No alphabet has yet been devised
        to explain it——
        ——the letters refuse coherence.
Unruly.

      ~⊃

The fish of this world, if they could talk,
and who knows if they can't, maybe
they have long philosophical conversations under
water, as they try to survive, always a reason for speech——
would tell us that the last fish of West Africa are filled
with the bones, cartilage, delicate

metatarsals, the still-wet liver, the mushroom hearts
of yesteryear's slaves—but that doesn't matter
don't worry, the fish have been fished,
the African's starve, and we sit at dinner, the unruly alphabet
pressed under our linen napkins, my dress
soaked and salty, your cufflinks, dry.

Fourth Veil

~⌒~

Our words catch in her grille;
but her body's inscribed with henna,
& my fingers, inked.

~⌒~

No flattens against you like a moth,
a hand, a cloth; *no* crawls into your eyes, splitting
your face—hers is covered to remind you of who
you are—what you will not see.

~⌒~

a doorway
to the *away-from*—

Decanted

The tangerines are tender this year
Their stems tremble in uneasy times
Yesterday, the wisteria turned
Today the sun roils inside the sea.

Disconsolate, the lemons lure the dark
The lackluster, the lonely, the lost
And just now jerusalem's thorn juts
Itself into someone else's skin.

The yellowed leaf is loosened like
Desire done; a note decanted
Color collapses, a mute curtain
Of gold flutters gorgeous to ground.

We ask who we are and why we are
And when we will be what we will be
But when the frost is laid out like lace
Life cloisters, and, in such closing, lasts.

Fifth Veil

～

Defiant, she covers
her face. Rebellious,
she billows out, a sheet loosened from its line.

～

Sky is everywhere: blue *burqa* sky.

Spring

(Ghazal)

There is a wellspring in us.
A green infinite *thing* in us.

The catmint opens to its hour, then the marigold soon after; the hawkweed turns
and follows. They make a clock of all that's manifold to wring a mercy from us.

Evening primroses release their scent to help the sun go down at dusk;
in darkness they whirl all whiteness and outline the hint of wing for us.

I hear it. Do you? The air "of silence and honeysuckle"?
If only we could be a bowl——to gather everything in us.

A billion years, two-layer hemisphere, two-layer sphere, eerie
Apis mellifera. We, honey gatherers, beelining: just human, us.

"A god can do it." Find our crevice and curve, that bottom
place where we are numb. Prayer is only this: Bring us to us.

I say "us" and "we" but who is that? Am I a *true image* really?
"Man's mind is cleft." I love, and aim bowstring, arrow——at us.

Sixth Veil

⌒

She sees through a window.
I look back at a mirror.
A one-way mirror——to interrogate
me.

⌒

Don't assume.
There is a divide: Who speaks? Who listens?

Snow In April

A Ghazal for Manadel al-Jamadi

White presses green against the wall: brute snow in April.
Green is annexed; no black dirt, no roots: snow in April.

A ghost interrogates what's hidden—its whiteness warps us all.
Nothing natural—all flowers being mute—under snow of April.

Gray fills the sky with itself, all foreign color smothered. What is
solid disappears—inside the frost—a chute—snow in April.

Has my flock of flowers died? An ambush, a bullet-shot
of cold. Undone beneath the snow, what's truth, in April?

The hawk-moth grows tipsy sipping nectar, hallucinates into walls:
Fragile datura opens—once—its parachute, in snow, in April.

It takes 4 days to break (a flower)—"16 hours of light & music & then
4 hours off." But Veronica, what's this—a single shoot? Ah, snow, but *April*.

Seventh Veil

Twist of cloth. One finger holds it
closed.

Unveiled

I   the wide-mouthed Queen   utterly named

          Sister   to the calamitous   One Who Outlasts

I was Queen and Mother   My infant's wrapping cloth

        I wove into crown

O Fanna'théna!

      Our greenfroth land   Our robe   is no longer

      Turmoil   war and drought   there was

and death   In thirst   we called out

for the pyre   Hear me!   My people

      You who are   look at my face   and   Remember

Whirling   the God came

September 11, 2009

Notes:

Poem of Three:

The year is a wound; the year is a yoke——from *The Whorehouse*, Badr Shakir al-Sayyab, Iraqi poet.

We are not going to give back any territory. Not in Baghdad.——said by United States Maj Gen. Jeffrey W. Hammond.

At the end of sorrow is a door is a paraphrase of *At the end of my suffering was a door*, Louise Glück, *Wild Iris*, American poet.

Voices:

I am working under the voices of fire, said by Palestinian Shareef Surhan during the Winter 08 bombing of Gaza by Israel, found in *epalestine.com*

Photo/syn/thesis:

This poem is a response to one of the photos of torture taken at Abu Ghraib, in particular the one of Private First Class Lynndie England holding a leash attached to the neck of a bound and naked prisoner, nicknamed "Gus" by the U.S. soldiers. The photo was taken by Corporal Charles Graner, Lynndie England 's superior officer and lover. http://www.newyorker.com/archive/2004/05/10/040510fa_fact

. . . there were meadows covered with human skin under the Arabian moon——from *The Arab Apocalypse*, Etel Adnan, Lebanese poet.

The dark thick fabric of the underneath——from *History* in the *Region of Unlikeness*, Jorie Graham, American poet.

Vocabulary of Silence:

Behold . . . here are my good . . . dead rising!, paraphrased from *The War Works Hard*, Dunya Mikhael, Iraqi poet.

Born between river and river, born between sword and sword——paraphrased from *Postcards from Hajj Omranem*, Saadi Yussef, Iraqi poet.

The City: Juárez, 2010

For more than a decade, the cities of Chihuahua and Juárez, near the US-Mexico border, have been killing fields, the site of over 400 unsolved murders of young girls and women. Many of the bodies have been found in the desert. A significant number of victims work in the *maquiladora* sweatshops. See, *takenbythesky.net*.

Santa Muerte: Saint Death. Santa Muerte generally appears as a skeletal figure, clad in a long robe and carrying one or more objects, usually a scythe and a globe; popular and widespread in Juárez, Mexico.

Dominus Vobiscum: From the Catholic Latin Mass, "May the Lord be with you."

Voces sin eco: Spanish——Voices without echo.

Letter damaged in transit:

This is a "found" poem. Most of its content is taken from transcripts posted on Alternet from over 50 combat veterans of Iraq interviewed in an article posted July 13, 07 by Chris Hedges and Laila al-Arian, in the *Nation* magazine. See: (www.alternet.org/story/56761)

For Fallujah:

Because poems are, after all, dialogues between the song of man and the silences of God——from *Some Notes on Silence*, by Jorie Graham, in *By Herself*, edited by Molly McQuade.

At some point we may be the only ones left. That's ok with me. We are America——quote by George W. Bush from *American Apocalypse*, in *The Nation*, by Robert Jay Lifton. (http://www.factnet.org/American_Apocalypse.html)

Allahu Akbar! "God is Great," recited five times daily in Islam's Call to Prayer.

Bombs rob night of its color——from *State of Siege*, Mahmoud Darwish, Palestinian poet.
A red that kindles in the body——from *Late Afternoon on the Shatt al-'Arab*, Badr Shakir al-Sayyab, Iraqi poet.

Birth(ing) Word:

babyblue exhalation of the one god; out of what ceases into what is ceasing—from *No Le Me Tangere*, in *The End of Beauty*, by Jorie Graham, American poet.

". . . on the palms of My hands have I graven thee."—from *The Epistle of Paul to the Galatians*, New Testament.

Axis Mundi: the sacred pole of the world, cosmic axis, world axis, the navel of the world connecting the upper and lower levels, meeting point. See Mercea Eliade, *Images & Symbols*.

Poppy13:

Somniferum—Latin—that which induces sleep.

Mazur-i-Sharif, Badakhstan, Jalalabad—cities in Afghanistan.

Sumeria:

Sumer was a collection of city-states around the Lower Tigris and Euphrates rivers in what is now southern Iraq.

After:

Lines in quotes are from *Call Me Ishmael Tonight, A Book of Ghazals*, by Agha Shahid Ali, Kashmiri-American poet.

Bop(K)not: Juba! Juba!

The *Bop* is a poetic form of recent invention, created by African-American poet Afaa Michael Weaver.

". . . the girl running to me . . . napalm-photo-run" refers to the iconic photo of the naked nine-year-old Vietnamese child Kim Phúc running down the road, her back burned with napalm, in the aftermath of the bombing of her village of Trang Bang on June 8, 1972, during the U.S. war against Vietnam. Associated press photographer Nick Ut earned a Pulitzer Prize for his photograph. In an interview many years later, Kim Phúc recalled yelling, "Nonq qua, nong qua" (too hot, too hot").

Spring *(A Ghazal):*

All quotes are from *Sonnets to Orpheus*, Rainer Maria Rilke, translated by Chris Brandt, by permission of the author.

True Image—translation of the name Veronica.

Snow in April:

Manadel al-Jamadi was a prisoner at Abu Ghraib. "Ghosts", or un-uniformed operatives, beat him to death; American soldiers tried to hide his death by removing him from the prison in a stretcher, with an IV attached. See *The New Yorker*, Nov. 14, 2005, article by Jane Mayer.

"16 hours of light & music & then 4 hours off." This is a quote from Guantanamo soldiers on how to 'break a prisoner' (same source).

Selected Bibliography

POETRY

The Arab Apocalypse, Etel Adnan, The Post-Apollo Press

The Pages of Day and Night, Adonis, translated by Samuel Hazo, Northwestern University Press

The Far Mosque, Kazim Ali, Alice James Books

A Nostalgist's Map of America, Agha Shahid Ali, Norton

Call Me Ishmael Tonight—A Book of Ghazals, Agha Shahid Ali, Norton

Miracle Maker, Fadhil al-Azzawi, Translated by Khaled Mattawa, Boa

The Sadness of Others, Hayan Charara, Carnegie Mellon Press

Why Did You Leave the Horse Alone, Mahmoud Darwish, translated by Jeffrey Sacks, Archipelago Books

Sin, the Selected Poems of Forugh Farrokhzad, translated by Sholeh Wolpé, University of Arkansas Press

The Lives of Rain, Nathalie Handal, Interlink

Into It, Lawrence Joseph, Farrar, Straus and Giroux

The World's Embrace, Selected Poems, Abdellatif Laaabi, Translations by Anne George, Edris Makward, Victor Reinking and Pierre Joris, City Lights Books

ANTHOLOGIES

Anthology of Modern Palestinian Literature, Editor Salma Khadra Jayyusi, Columbia University Press

Mahmoud Darwish—Exile's Poet, Editor Khamis Nassar Rahman, Olive Branch Press

Inclined to Speak: An Anthology of Contemporary Arab-American Poets, editor Hayan Charara, University of Arkansas

Iraqi Poetry Today, Editor Saadi Simawe, Modern Poetry in Translation

Modern Arabic Poetry, editor Salma Khadra Jayyusi, Columbia University Press

Placing the Poet—Badr Shakir al-Sayyab and Post Colonial Iraq, by Terri Deyoung, Suny University Press

Poems of Arab Andalusia, translated by Cola Franzen, City Light Books

The Poetry of Arab Women: A Contemporary Anthology, editor Nathalie Handal, Interlink Press

Ravishing DisUnities: Real Ghazals in English, editor Agha Shahid Ali, Wesleyan University Press

Songs of Love and War: Afghan Women's Poetry, editor Sayd Bahodine Majrouh, translated by Marjolin de Jager, Other Press, NY

Victims of the Map, A Bilingual Anthology of Arabic Poetry: Adonis, Mahmoud Dariwsh, Samih al-Qasim, translated by Abdullah al-Udhari, Saqi Publishers

NON-FICTION

After the Last Sky: Palestinian Lives, Edward W. Said, Columbia University Press

Culture and Imperialism, Edward W. Said, Alfred A. Knoph, NY

The Edward Said Reader, Editors Moustafa Bayoumi and Andrew Rubin, Vintage Books

Orientalism, Edward W. Said, Vintage Books

Representations of the Intellectual, Edward W. Said, Vintage Books

NON-FICTION CONTINUED

Crimes of War—Iraq, Editors Richard Falk, Irene Gendzier, Robert Jay Lifton, Nation Books

Every War Has Two Losers, William Stafford on Peace and War, editor Kim Stafford, Milkweed Editions

The Fire This Time: US War Crimes in the Gulf, Ramsey Clark, International Action Center

Gandhi on Non-Violence: A Section from the Writings of Mahatma Gandhi, editor Thomas Merton, New Directions Paperback

The Girard Reader, edited by James G. Williams, Herder & Herder Books

Ghost Wars, Steve Coll, Penguin Books

One of the Guys, Women as Aggressors and Torturers, editor Tara McKelvey, Seal Press

The Punishment of Virtue: Inside Afghanistan After the Taliban, Sarah Chayes, The Penguin Press

Standard Operating Procedure, Phillip Gourevitch and Errol Morris, The Penguin Press

Swimming Up the Tigris: Real Life Encounters with Iraq, Barbara Nimri Aziz, University Press of Florida

Trauma and Recovery: The Aftermath of Violence—from domestic abuse to political terror, Judith Herman, M.D., Basic Books

War is a Force That Gives Us Meaning, Chris Hedges, Public Affairs Press

Biographical Note

Veronica Golos was co winner of the 16th annual Nicholas Roerich Poetry Prize (Story Line Press) for her book *A Bell Buried Deep* (to be re-issued by Red Hen Press), and is the author of *Vocabulary of Silence* (Red Hen Press, 2011). Golos has been an award winning curator and teacher for *Poets & Writers*, Poet's House and 92nd St Y/Makor in New York City, and her work has been published and anthologized nationally and internationally, as well as adapted for theatrical productions in New York City's Theatre Ro Row and the Claremont Theological Seminary in California. A long time political activist, her poetry was the centerpiece of *My Land is Me*, a four-artist multimedia exhibit in Taos, NM that questioned the western view of the Veil. Presently, she lives in Taos, New Mexico with her husband, writer David Pérez.

To contact for readings, presentations, and performances: vgdp@aol.com

For more of Veronica Golos' work, visit: http://veronicagolos.wordpress.com

CPSIA information can be obtained
at www.ICGtesting.com
Printed in the USA
BVOW10n2053280717

490557BV00007B/17/P